Beginner's Guide to
Crochet Motifs

LEISURE ARTS, INC. • Maumelle, Arkansas

EDITORIAL STAFF

Vice President of Editorial: Susan White Sullivan
Creative Art Director: Katherine Laughlin
Publications Director: Leah Lampirez
Technical Writer/Editor: Linda A. Daley
Associate Technical Editors: Sarah J. Green and
 Lois J. Long
Editorial Writer: Susan Frantz Wiles
Art Category Manager: Lora Puls
Graphic Artist: Jacqueline Breazeal
Prepress Technician: Stephanie Johnson
Contributing Photographer: Jason Masters
Contributing Photo Stylist: Lori Wenger

BUSINESS STAFF

President and Chief Executive Officer: Fred F. Pruss
Senior Vice President of Operations: Jim Dittrich
Vice President of Retail Sales: Martha Adams
Vice President of Mass Market Sales:
 Bob Bewighouse
Vice President of Technology and Planning:
 Laticia Mull Dittrich
Controller: Tiffany P. Childers
Information Technology Director: Brian Roden
Director of E-Commerce: Mark Hawkins
Manager of E-Commerce: Robert Young

ISBN-13: 978-1-4647-1267-8

Once you learn to make and join motifs, you can "build" all kinds of projects!

This book introduces you to a variety of motif shapes and shows you how to use them to make afghans, baby blankets, shawls, scarves and cowls. Camera icons 🎥 let you know when there are free online videos to help you learn the techniques. Get ready for a lifetime of creative crochet!

Meet the Designer

Photo by Heather Weston

With more than 800 knit and crochet designs in print, Melissa Leapman is one of the most widely published American designers working today.

She began her design career by freelancing for leading ready-to-wear design houses in New York City, as well as working on commission for top yarn companies to create designs promoting their new and existing yarns each season. Her ability to quickly develop fully envisioned garments put her skills in great demand.

Through the years, Melissa's patterns have appeared in dozens of nationally known magazines, while her books and classes on knitting and crochet are consistently popular with the public. Melissa has been a featured guest on numerous television shows, is a popular guest blogger, and is the host of several Leisure Arts knitting and crocheting DVDs.

Nationally, her designs have been featured in numerous magazines, and her workshops on knitting and crochet are consistently popular with crafters of all skill levels. She has taught at major events such as STITCHES, Vogue Knitting LIVE, and The Knitting Guild Association conferences, as well as at hundreds of yarn shops and local guild events across the country.

To find more of Melissa's exciting designs, visit LeisureArts.com, "like" Melissa's Facebook page, and join her group (Melissa Leapman Rocks) on Ravelry.com.

6

26

12

32

18

38

Beginner's Guide To
CROCHET MOTIFS

Have you admired traditional crocheted motifs but been afraid to give them a try? Here's your chance to add this fun—and deceptively simple—crochet technique to your skill set.

When you break it down to basics, a motif is simply a miniature design, separate and complete in itself, although usually made in multiples and joined into larger projects. Worked in rounds, they can be any shape, from circles and squares to triangles, hexagons, octagons, rectangles, and other geometric shapes.

Motifs with equal-size flat sides fit together nicely, but circles and some other shapes will have gaps when the motifs are placed side by side. These gaps may be left open, for a lacy effect, or filled in with smaller motifs or filling stitches.

With this book and the free online technique videos that support it, you'll learn to make different styles of creative motifs and incorporate them into beautiful and useful projects ranging from fashion accessories to afghans for baby and home.

You'll also learn several joining methods. Traditional whipstitching is explained, plus no-sew techniques for connecting motifs as you finish crocheting one and begin another!

Let's start exploring....

Getting Started

The quickest and simplest way to learn about crochet motifs is to start with a basic motif and build your skills a little at a time. Many beginners find the traditional granny square to be an easy motif, so this book starts with a granny square afghan. However, any of the motifs and projects should be equally easy, so take your pick! Two bonus colorways are shown with each project to show you how different the motif looks when the color placement is changed.

Supplies

To crochet motifs, you'll only need basic supplies such as medium weight yarn and crochet hooks. Since the gauge of your stitches and rounds is important to ensure that your finished project is the desired size, you'll want a tape measure, too. A yarn needle is also used to weave in yarn ends, as well as to sew motifs together.

Traditional Granny
Afghan

While making this afghan, you will learn how to:

- Begin your granny square with a chain ring

- Join to the first stitch when working in rounds

- Join a new color of yarn

- Whipstitch the granny squares together through the back loop

Finished Size:

Approximately 51¼" x 63¼" (130 cm x 160.5 cm)

—————— **SHOPPING LIST** ——————

Yarn (Medium Weight)

[3.5 ounces, 170 yards

(100 grams, 156 meters) per skein]:

☐ Color A (White) - 7 skeins

☐ Color B (Red) - 5 skeins

☐ Color C (Blue) - 3 skeins

Crochet Hook

☐ Size I (5.5 mm) **or** size needed for gauge

Additional Supplies

☐ Yarn needle

GAUGE INFORMATION

Each Granny Square = 6" (15.25 cm)

Gauge Swatch: 4" (10 cm)

Work Granny Square through Rnd 3: 36 dc and 12 sps.

INSTRUCTIONS
Granny Square (Make 80)

One of the easiest ways to begin a motif or square is with a ring.

With Color C, ch 4; ▐▌ join with slip st to first ch made to form a ring *(Fig. 1)*.

Fig. 1

Rnd 1 (Right side)**:** Ch 3 **(counts as first dc, now and throughout)**, ▐▌ 2 dc in ring *(Figs. 2a & b)*, ch 2, (3 dc in ring, ch 2) 3 times; ▐▌ join with slip st to first dc *(Fig. 2c)*: 12 dc and 4 corner ch-2 sps.

Fig. 2a

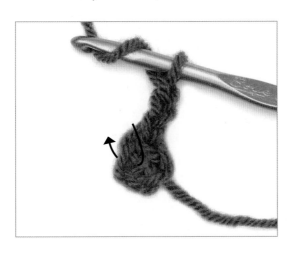

Fig. 2b

Fig. 2c

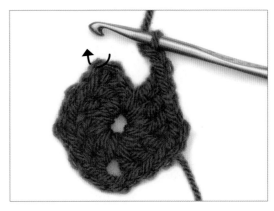

Note: Loop a short piece of yarn around any stitch to mark Rnd 1 as **right** side.

Rnd 2: Slip st in next 2 dc and in next corner ch-2 sp, ch 3, (2 dc, ch 2, 3 dc) in same corner sp, ch 1, skip next 3 dc, ★ (3 dc, ch 2, 3 dc) in next corner ch-2 sp, ch 1, skip next 3 sts; repeat from ★ 2 times **more**; join with slip st to first dc, finish off: 24 dc and 8 sps.

Your choice of yarn colors for the rounds of the granny square can result in vastly different looks.

Rnd 3: With **right** side facing, 🎥 join Color A with slip st in any corner ch-2 sp *(Figs. 3a & b)*; ch 3, (2 dc, ch 2, 3 dc) in same corner sp, ch 1, skip next 3 dc, 3 dc in next ch-1 sp, ch 1, skip next 3 dc, ★ (3 dc, ch 2, 3 dc) in next corner ch-2 sp, ch 1, skip next 3 dc, 3 dc in next ch-1 sp, ch 1, skip next 3 dc; repeat from ★ 2 times **more**; join with slip st to first dc: 36 dc and 12 sps.

Fig. 3b

Fig. 3a

Rnd 4: Slip st in next 2 dc and in next corner ch-2 sp, ch 3, (2 dc, ch 2, 3 dc) in same corner sp, ch 1, skip next 3 dc, (3 dc in next ch-1 sp, ch 1, skip next 3 dc) twice, ★ (3 dc, ch 2, 3 dc) in next corner ch-2 sp, ch 1, skip next 3 dc, (3 dc in next ch-1 sp, ch 1, skip next 3 sts) twice; repeat from ★ 2 times **more**; join with slip st to first dc, finish off: 48 dc and 16 sps.

Rnd 5: With **right** side facing, join Color B with slip st in any corner ch-2 sp; ch 3, (2 dc, ch 2, 3 dc) in same corner sp, ch 1, skip next 3 dc, (3 dc in next ch-1 sp, ch 1, skip next 3 dc) 3 times, ★ (3 dc, ch 2, 3 dc) in next corner ch-2 sp, ch 1, skip next 3 dc, (3 dc in next ch-1 sp, ch 1, skip next 3 dc) 3 times; repeat from ★ 2 times **more**; join with slip st to first dc, finish off: 60 dc and 20 sps.

Assembly

For illustration purposes, we are showing how to sew our squares together using a contrasting color.

🎥 Whipstitch 2 squares together as follows:
Place Squares with **right** side facing and edges matching. With Color B and beginning in second ch of first corner, sew through both pieces once to secure the beginning of the seam (*Fig. 4a*), leaving an ample yarn end to weave in later. Working through **back** loops of each stitch on **both** pieces, insert the needle from **right** to **left** through the first stitch (*Fig. 4b*) and pull yarn through, ★ insert the needle from **right** to **left** through the next stitch and pull yarn through; repeat from ★ across ending in first ch of next corner.

TIP: When whipstitching squares together, maintain a relaxed tension on the sewing yarn and do not pull the stitches too tightly. If possible, use the yarn tails for sewing, to reduce the number of ends to be woven in later.

Fig. 4a

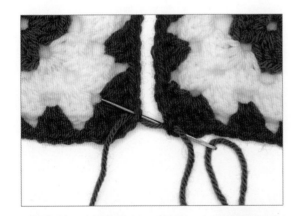

Fig. 4b

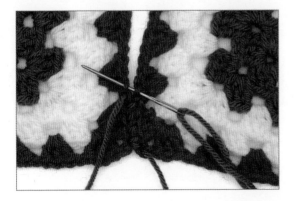

Whipstitch remaining Squares together, forming 8 vertical strips of 10 squares each.
Whipstitch strips together in same manner.

Edging

Rnd 1: With **right** side facing, join Color B with slip st in any corner ch-2 sp; ch 3, (2 dc, ch 2, 3 dc) in same sp, ch 1, skip next 3 dc, (3 dc in next ch-1 sp, ch 1, skip next 3 dc) 4 times, ★ † dc in next sp, dc in joining and in next sp, ch 1, skip next 3 dc, (3 dc in next ch-1 sp, ch 1, skip next 3 dc) 4 times †, repeat from † to † across to next corner ch-2 sp, (3 dc, ch 2, 3 dc) in corner sp, ch 1, skip next 3 dc, (3 dc in next ch-1 sp, ch 1, skip next 3 dc) 4 times; repeat from ★ 2 times **more**, then repeat from † to † across; join with slip st to first dc: 552 dc and 184 sps.

Rnd 2: Ch 1, sc in same st as joining and in next 2 dc, 3 sc in corner ch-2 sp, ★ sc in next 3 dc, (sc in next ch-1 sp, sc in next 3 dc) across to next corner ch-2 sp, 3 sc in corner sp; repeat from ★ 2 times **more**, (sc in next 3 dc and in next ch-1 sp) across; join with slip st to first sc, finish off.

Amish Hexagon
Afghan

While making this afghan, you will learn how to:

- Begin your hexagon motif by working into one chain of the beginning chain

- Join to the first stitch when working in rounds

- Join a new color of yarn

- Whipstitch the motifs together through the back loop

Finished Size:
Approximately 44" x 60" (112 cm x 152.5 cm)

—— SHOPPING LIST ——

Yarn (Medium Weight)

[3.5 ounces, 170 yards
(100 grams, 156 meters) per skein]:

☐ Color A (Dusty Purple) - 8 skeins
☐ Color B (Magenta) - 4 skeins
☐ Color C (Dusty Rose) - 2 skeins

Crochet Hook

☐ Size I (5.5 mm) **or** size needed for gauge

Additional Supplies

☐ Yarn needle

GAUGE INFORMATION

Each Motif = 4" (10 cm)
(from straight edge to straight edge)
Gauge Swatch: 4" (10 cm)
Work One Motif: 42 dc and 6 ch-2 sps.

INSTRUCTIONS
Motif (Make 188)

Some motifs and squares begin with a chain and all of the stitches of the first round are worked into the first chain made. With this Motif, the skipped chains become the first stitch of the round as well as a chain space once the round is joined.

Rnd 1 (Right side)**:** With Color C, ch 6, (dc, ch 2) 5 times in sixth ch from hook *(Fig. 5a)*; join with slip st to third ch of beginning ch-6 *(Fig. 5b)*, finish off: 6 ch-2 sps.

Fig. 5a

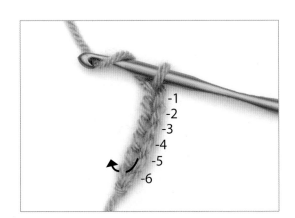

Fig. 5b

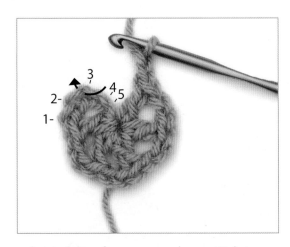

Note: Loop a short piece of yarn around any stitch to mark Rnd 1 as **right** side.

Rnd 2: With **right** side facing, join Color B with slip st in any ch-2 sp *(Figs. 6a & b)*; ch 3 **(counts as first dc, now and throughout)**, 2 dc in same sp, ch 2, (3 dc in next ch-2 sp, ch 2) around; join with slip st to first dc, finish off: 18 dc and 18 ch-2 sps.

Fig. 6a

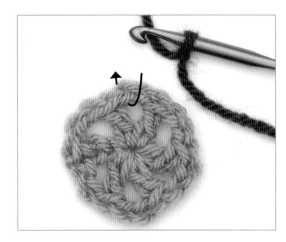

Fig. 6b

Rnd 3: With **right** side facing, join Color A with slip st in any ch-2 sp; ch 3, (dc, ch 2, 2 dc) in same sp, dc in next 3 dc, ★ (2 dc, ch 2, 2 dc) in next ch-2 sp, dc in next 3 dc; repeat from ★ around; join with slip st to first dc, finish off: 42 dc and 6 ch-2 sps.

Assembly

For illustration purposes, we are showing how to sew our motifs together using a contrasting color.

Fig. 7a

📹 Whipstitch 2 motifs together as follows:
Place Motifs with **right** side facing and edges matching. With Color A and beginning in second ch of first ch-2, sew through both pieces once to secure the beginning of the seam *(Fig. 7a)*, leaving an ample yarn end to weave in later. Working through **back** loops of each stitch on **both** pieces, insert the needle from **right** to **left** through the first stitch *(Fig. 7b)* and pull yarn through, ★ insert the needle from **right** to **left** through the next stitch and pull yarn through; repeat from ★ across ending in first ch of next ch-2.

Fig. 7b

TIP: When whipstitching squares together, maintain a relaxed tension on the sewing yarn and do not pull the stitches too tightly. If possible, use the yarn tails for sewing, to reduce the number of ends to be woven in later.

Notice how the dark and light colors make the features of the motif stand out or fade into the background.

Referring to Assembly Diagram, whipstitch remaining Motifs together, forming 7 vertical strips of 14 motifs each and 6 vertical strips of 15 motifs each. Whipstitch strips together in same manner.

ASSEMBLY DIAGRAM

Blooming Squares
Baby Afghan

While making this afghan, you will learn how to:

- Begin your square by making an adjustable loop

- Join to the first stitch when working in rounds

- Join a new color of yarn

- Work a no-sew joining to connect your squares together as you crochet the last round

Finished Size:

Approximately 36" (91.5 cm) square

SHOPPING LIST

Yarn (Medium Weight)

[3.5 ounces, 170 yards
(100 grams, 156 meters) per skein]:

☐ Color A (Melon) - 3 skeins

☐ Color B (Lt Green) - 3 skeins

☐ Color C (Yellow) - 2 skeins

Crochet Hook

☐ Size I (5.5 mm) **or** size needed for gauge

GAUGE INFORMATION

Each Square = 5" (12.5 cm) square

Gauge Swatch: 3" (7.5 cm) diameter

Work First Square through Rnd 2: 8 Clusters
and 8 ch-4 sps.

STITCH GUIDE

BEGINNING CLUSTER (uses one sc)

Ch 3, ★ YO, insert hook in sc indicated, YO and
pull up a loop, YO and draw through 2 loops on
hook; repeat from ★ once **more**, YO and draw
through all 3 loops on hook.

CLUSTER (uses one sc)

★ YO, insert hook in sc indicated, YO and pull
up a loop, YO and draw through 2 loops on
hook; repeat from ★ 2 times **more**, YO and
draw through all 4 loops on hook.

INSTRUCTIONS
First Square

To make the center opening on your motif or square as small as possible, use an adjustable loop.

Rnd 1 (Right side): 🎥 To make an adjustable loop, wind Color C around two fingers to form a ring *(Fig. 8a)*, then slide yarn off fingers and grasp the strands at the top of the ring *(Fig. 8b)*.

Fig. 8a

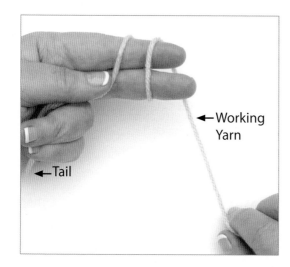

← Working Yarn

← Tail

Fig. 8b

Insert hook from **front** to **back** into the ring, pull up a loop, YO and draw through loop on hook to lock the ring *(Fig. 8c)*, ch 1, working around **both** strands, work 8 sc in ring, pull yarn tail to close *(Fig. 8d)*; 🎥 join with slip st to first sc *(Fig. 9)*, finish off.

Fig. 8c

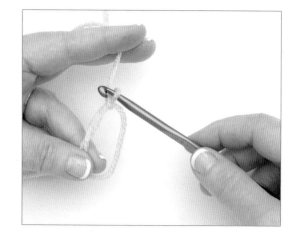

Fig. 8d

Fig. 9

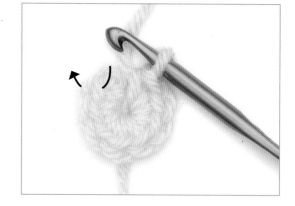

Note: Loop a short piece of yarn around any stitch to mark Rnd 1 as **right** side.

Rnd 2: With **right** side facing, 🎥 join Color A with slip st in any sc *(Figs. 10a & b)*; work beginning Cluster in same st, ch 4, (work Cluster in next sc, ch 4) around; join with slip st to top of beginning Cluster, finish off: 8 Clusters and 8 ch-4 sps.

Fig. 10a

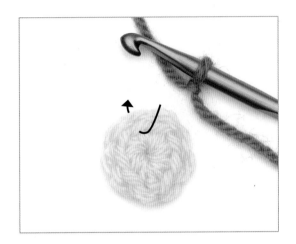

Fig. 10b

Rnd 3: With **right** side facing, join Color B with slip st in any ch-4 sp; ch 1, 4 sc in same sp, ch 1, (4 sc in next ch-4 sp, ch 1) around; join with slip st to first sc, do **not** finish off: 32 sc and 8 ch-1 sps.

Rnd 4: Ch 3 (**counts as first dc**), hdc in next sc, sc in next 2 sc, sc in next ch-1 sp and in next 2 sc, hdc in next sc, dc in next sc, (2 dc, ch 2, 2 dc) in next ch-1 sp, ★ dc in next sc, hdc in next sc, sc in next 2 sc, sc in next ch-1 sp and in next 2 sc, hdc in next sc, dc in next sc, (2 dc, ch 2, 2 dc) in next ch-1 sp; repeat from ★ 2 times **more**; join with slip st to first dc, finish off: 52 sts and 4 corner ch-2 sps.

Rnd 5: With **right** side facing, join Color C with slip st in any corner ch-2 sp; ch 1, (sc, ch 2, sc) in same corner sp, sc in next 13 sts, ★ (sc, ch 2, sc) in next corner ch-2 sp, sc in next 13 sts; repeat from ★ 2 times **more**; join with slip st to first sc, finish off: 60 sc and 4 corner ch-2 sps.

Rnd 6: With **right** side facing, join Color A with slip st in any corner ch-2 sp; ch 1, (sc, ch 5) twice in same corner sp, skip next 3 sc, (slip st in next sc, ch 5, skip next 3 sc) 3 times, ★ (sc, ch 5) twice in next corner ch-2 sp, skip next 3 sc, (slip st in next sc, ch 5, skip next 3 sc) 3 times; repeat from ★ 2 times **more**; join with slip st to first sc, finish off: 20 ch-5 sps.

Additional 35 Squares

📹 The method used to connect the Squares is a no-sew joining known as "join-as-you-go."

Work each remaining Square through Rnd 5 of First Square: 60 sc and 4 corner ch-2 sps.

Using Placement Diagram as a guide for Square placement and order, work a One- or Two-Side Joining, pages 24 and 25, to crochet Squares together across the last side(s) as Rnd 6 is worked. The first strip (Squares 1-6) will use the One-Side Joining only. The first square of each remaining strip will also be joined using the One-Side Joining (Squares 7, 13, 19, 25 & 31), while the remaining squares will be joined using the Two-Side Joining.

TIP: When joining corners where more than one Square meet, always join into the same stitch as previous joining.

PLACEMENT DIAGRAM

1	7	13	19	25	31
2	8	14	20	26	32
3	9	15	21	27	33
4	10	16	22	28	34
5	11	17	23	29	35
6	12	18	24	30	36

Plan your colors to accent specific areas of the square, such as the center or the last round.

Insert your hook from the **back** to the **front** through the space on the **adjacent Motif**, keeping the working yarn at the **back** of your hook.

ONE-SIDE JOINING

Rnd 6 (Joining rnd)**:** With **right** side facing, join Color A with slip st in any corner ch-2 sp; ch 1, (sc, ch 5) twice in same corner sp, skip next 3 sc, (slip st in next sc, ch 5, skip next 3 sc) 3 times, (sc, ch 5) twice in next corner ch-2 sp, skip next 3 sc, (slip st in next sc, ch 5, skip next 3 sc) 3 times, sc in next corner ch-2 sp, ch 2; holding Squares with **right** side facing, slip st in corner ch-5 sp on **adjacent Square** *(Fig. 11a)*, ch 2, sc in same corner sp on **new Square**, ch 2, slip st in next ch-5 sp on **adjacent Square**, ch 2, skip next 3 sc on **new Square**, [slip st in next sc *(Fig. 11b)*, ch 2, slip st in next ch-5 sp on **adjacent Square**, ch 2, skip next 3 sc on **new Square**] 3 times, sc in next corner ch-2 sp, ch 2, slip st in next corner ch-5 sp on **adjacent Square**, ch 2, sc in same corner sp on **new Square**, ch 5, skip next 3 sc, (slip st in next sc, ch 5, skip next 3 sc) 3 times; join with slip st to first sc, finish off: 20 ch-sps.

Fig. 11a

Fig. 11b

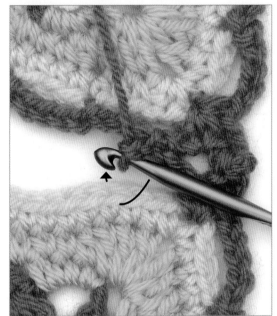

TWO-SIDE JOINING

Rnd 6 (Joining rnd)**:** With **right** side facing, join Color A with slip st in any corner ch-2 sp; ch 1, (sc, ch 5) twice in same corner sp, skip next 3 sc, (slip st in next sc, ch 5, skip next 3 sc) 3 times, sc in next corner ch-2 sp, ch 2; holding Squares with **right** side facing, slip st in corner ch-5 sp on **adjacent Square**, ch 2, sc in same corner sp on **new Square**, ★ ch 2, slip st in next ch-5 sp on **adjacent Square**, ch 2, skip next 3 sc on **new Square**, (slip st in next sc, ch 2, slip st in next ch-5 sp on **adjacent Square**, ch 2, skip next 3 sc on **new Square**) 3 times, sc in next corner ch-2 sp, ch 2, slip st in next corner ch-5 sp on **adjacent Square**, ch 2, sc in same corner sp on **new Square**; repeat from ★ once **more**, ch 5, skip next 3 sc, (slip st in next sc, ch 5, skip next 3 sc) 3 times; join with slip st to first sc, finish off: 20 ch-sps.

Edging

With **right** side facing, join Color A with slip st in any corner ch-5 sp; ch 1, (sc, ch 7, sc) in same corner sp, ★ † ch 5, (slip st in next ch-5 sp, ch 5) 4 times, [slip st in joining st, ch 5, (slip st in next ch-5 sp, ch 5) 4 times] across to next corner ch-5 sp †, (sc, ch 7, sc) in corner sp; repeat from ★ 2 times **more**, then repeat from † to † once; join with slip st to first sc, finish off.

This is how your squares will look when they have been joined together. The connected areas form a pattern of their own.

Autumn Mums
Shawl

While making this shawl, you will learn how to:

- Begin your motif by making an adjustable loop

- Join to the first stitch when working in rounds

- Work a no-sew joining to connect your motifs together as you crochet the round

- Follow a diagram for motif placement

 EASY +

Finished Size:

Approximately 22"w x 63¼"l (56 cm x 160.5 cm)

─── **SHOPPING LIST** ───

Yarn (Medium Weight) 🧶 **MEDIUM 4**

[3.5 ounces, 170 yards

(100 grams, 156 meters) per skein]:

☐ Color A (Brown) - 2 skeins

☐ Color B (Lt Blue) - 2 skeins

☐ Color C (Navy) - 2 skeins

☐ Color D (Lt Tan) - 2 skeins

Crochet Hook

☐ Size I (5.5 mm) **or** size needed for gauge

GAUGE INFORMATION

Gauge Swatch: 2¾" (7 cm) from
 corner to opposite corner

Work same as First Motif: 8 sc, 4 corner ch-9 sps, and 4 ch-7 sps (8 sps total).

INSTRUCTIONS
First Motif

Rnd 1 (Right side): 🎥 To make an adjustable loop, wind Color A around two fingers to form a ring *(Fig. 12a)*, then slide yarn off fingers and grasp the strands at the top of the ring *(Fig. 12b)*.

Fig. 12a

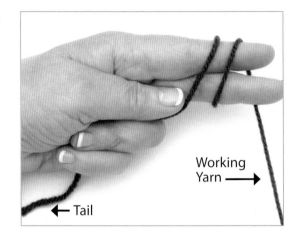

Working Yarn →

← Tail

Fig. 12b

Insert hook from **front** to **back** into the ring, pull up a loop, YO and draw through loop on hook to lock the ring *(Fig. 12c)*, ch 1, working around **both** strands,

★ sc in ring, ch 7, sc in ring, ch 9; repeat from ★ 3 times **more**, pull yarn tail to close *(Fig. 12d)*; 🎥 join with slip st to first sc *(Fig. 13)*, finish off: 8 sc, 4 corner ch-9 sps, and 4 ch-7 sps (8 sps total).

Fig. 12c

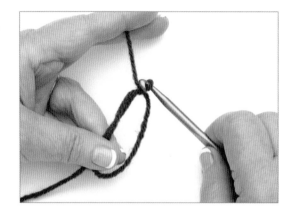

Fig. 12d

Fig. 13

Note: Loop a short piece of yarn around any stitch to mark Rnd 1 as **right** side.

Additional 336 Motifs

📹 The method used to connect the Motifs is a no-sew joining known as "join-as-you-go."

Using Diagram as a guide for color placement, work a One- or Two-Side Joining to crochet Motifs together in diagonal rows as Rnd 1 is worked.

When joining the second thru seventh rows of Motifs, join the second Motif to the previous diagonal row before joining the first Motif so that the entire side of the Motif is joined (3 points along one side).

Insert your hook from the **back** to the **front** through the center chain on the **adjacent Motif**, keeping the working yarn at the **back** of your hook.

TIP: When joining corners where more than one Motif meet, always join into the same ch as previous joining(s).

PLACEMENT DIAGRAM

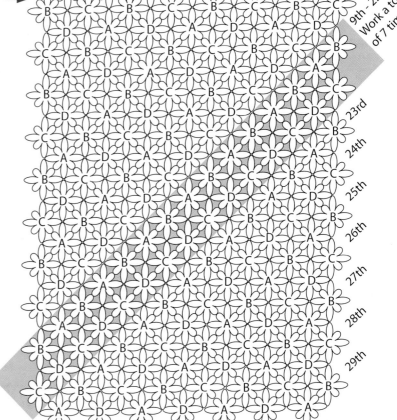

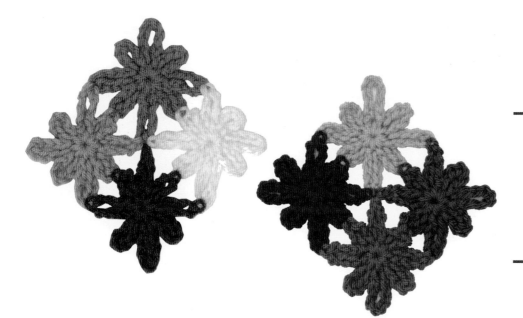

When planning your shawl, consider choosing seasonal colors, such as the spring and fall combinations shown here.

ONE-SIDE JOINING

Rnd 1 (Joining rnd)**:** Make an adjustable loop with next color *(Figs. 12a-c, page 29)*, ch 1, sc in ring, ch 7, sc in ring, ★ ch 9, sc in ring, ch 7, sc in ring; repeat from ★ once **more**, ch 4; holding Motifs with **right** side facing, slip st in center ch of corner ch-9 on **adjacent Motif** *(Fig. 14a)*, ch 4, sc in ring on **new Motif**, ch 3, slip st in center ch of next ch-7 on **adjacent Motif** *(Fig. 14b)*, ch 3, sc in ring on **new Motif**, ch 4, slip st in center ch of corner ch-9 on **adjacent Motif**, ch 4, pull yarn tail to close; join with slip st to first sc on **new Motif**, finish off: 8 sc, 4 corner ch-9 sps, and 4 ch-7 sps (8 sps total).

Fig. 14a

Fig. 14b

TWO-SIDE JOINING

Rnd 1 (Joining rnd)**:** Make an adjustable loop with next color *(Figs. 12a-c, page 29)*, ch 1, sc in ring, ch 7, sc in ring, ch 9, sc in ring, ch 7, sc in ring, ch 4; holding Motifs with **right** side facing, slip st in center ch of corner ch-9 on **adjacent Motif**, ch 4, ★ sc in ring on **new Motif**, ch 3, slip st in center ch of next ch-7 on **adjacent Motif**, ch 3, sc in ring on **new Motif**, ch 4, slip st in center ch of corner ch-9 on **adjacent Motif**, ch 4; repeat from ★ once **more**, pull yarn tail to close; join with slip st to first sc on **new Motif**, finish off: 8 sc, 4 corner ch-9 sps, and 4 ch-7 sps (8 sps total).

This is how your motifs will look when the tips of the petals have been joined.

Frilly Circles
Scarf

While making this scarf, you will learn how to:

- Begin your motif by making an adjustable loop

- Join to the first stitch when working in rounds

- Work a no-sew joining to connect your motifs together as you crochet the round

- Follow a diagram for motif placement

Finished Size:

Approximately 6¾"w x 66¼"l (17 cm x 168.5 cm)

── SHOPPING LIST ──

Yarn (Medium Weight)

[3.5 ounces, 170 yards

(100 grams, 156 meters) per skein]:

☐ Color A (Bright Purple) - 1 skein

☐ Color B (Blue) - 1 skein

☐ Color C (Lt Blue) - 1 skein

☐ Color D (Purple) - 1 skein

Crochet Hook

☐ Size I (5.5 mm) **or** size needed for gauge

GAUGE INFORMATION

Gauge Swatch: 2¼" (5.75 cm) diameter

Work same as First Motif: 12 Picots.

INSTRUCTIONS
First Motif

Rnd 1 (Right side): 🎥 To make an adjustable loop, wind Color A around two fingers to form a ring *(Fig. 15a)*, then slide yarn off fingers and grasp the strands at the top of the ring *(Fig. 15b)*.

Fig. 15a

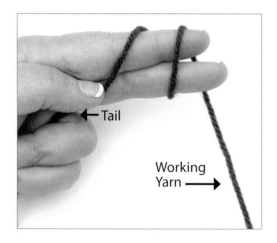

Fig. 15b

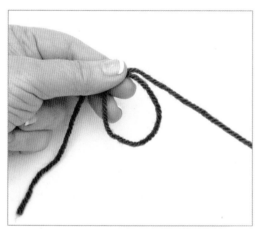

Fig. 15c

Fig. 15d

Fig. 16

Insert hook from **front** to **back** into the ring, pull up a loop, YO and draw through loop on hook to lock the ring *(Fig. 15c)*, ch 6, slip st in third ch from hook (**Picot made**), working around **both** strands, ★ dc in ring, ch 3, slip st in third ch from hook (**Picot made**); repeat from ★ 10 times **more**, pull yarn tail to close *(Fig. 15d)*; 🎥 join with slip st to third ch of beginning ch-6 *(Fig. 16)*, finish off: 12 Picots.

Note: Loop a short piece of yarn around any stitch to mark Rnd 1 as **right** side.

Second Motif

🎥 The method used to connect the Motifs is a no-sew joining known as "join-as-you-go."

Insert your hook from the **back** to the **front** through the ch-sp of any Picot on the **adjacent Motif**, keeping the working yarn at the **back** of your hook.

Rnd 1 (Joining rnd)**:** Make an adjustable loop with Color B *(Figs. 15a-c, page 35)*, ch 6, slip st in third ch from hook (**Picot made**), dc in ring, ★ ch 3, slip st in third ch from hook (**Picot made**), dc in ring; repeat from ★ 9 times **more**, ch 1; holding Motifs with **right** side facing, slip st in ch-sp of any Picot on **First Motif** *(Fig. 17a)*, pull yarn tail to close, ch 1, slip st in next ch on **Second Motif** to form last Picot *(Fig. 17b)*; join with slip st to third ch of beginning ch-6, finish off: 12 Picots.

Fig. 17a

Fig. 17b

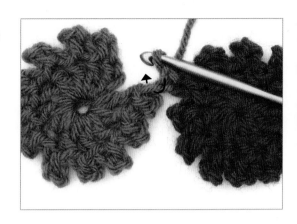

Remaining 80 Motifs

Alternating a row of 2 Motifs with a row of 3 Motifs, and using Diagram as a guide for color placement, work a Two- or Three-Side Joining to crochet Motifs together as Rnd 1 is worked. On rows containing 3 Motifs, work the center Motif first, then work the Motifs on each side of it.

PLACEMENT DIAGRAM

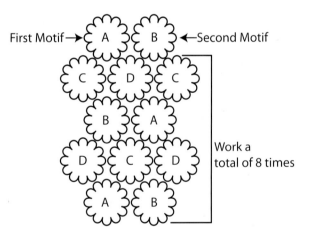

First Motif → A   B ← Second Motif

C   D   C

B   A

D   C   D   } Work a total of 8 times

A   B

Continue inserting your hook from the **back** to the **front** through the ch-sp of Picot indicated on the **adjacent Motif**, keeping the working yarn at the **back** of your hook.

When planning your scarf colors, think about how the colors of the joined motifs could form subtle patterns of circles or stripes.

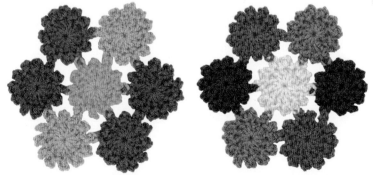

This is how your motifs will look when joined. Notice that only certain picots are connected.

TWO-SIDE JOINING

Rnd 1 (Joining rnd)**:** Make an adjustable loop with next color *(Figs. 15a-c, page 35)*, ch 6, slip st in third ch from hook (**Picot made**), dc in ring, ★ ch 3, slip st in third ch from hook (**Picot made**), dc in ring; repeat from ★ 7 times **more**, ch 1; holding Motifs with **right** side facing, skip one Picot **before** joining on **adjacent Motif** and slip st in ch-sp of next Picot (second Picot **before** joining) *(Fig. 18a)*, ch 1, slip st in next ch on **new Motif** to form Picot, dc in ring, ch 3, slip st in third ch from hook (**Picot made**), dc in ring, ch 1, skip joining and next Picot on **adjacent Motif** and slip st in ch-sp of next Picot (second Picot **after** joining) *(Fig. 18b)*, pull yarn tail to close, ch 1, slip st in next ch on **new Motif** to form last Picot; join with slip st to third ch of beginning ch-6, finish off: 12 Picots.

THREE-SIDE JOINING

Rnd 1 (Joining rnd)**:** Make an adjustable loop with next color *(Figs. 15a-c, page 35)*, ch 6, slip st in third ch from hook (**Picot made**), dc in ring, ★ ch 3, slip st in third ch from hook (**Picot made**), dc in ring; repeat from ★ 5 times **more**, ch 1; holding Motifs with **right** side facing, skip one Picot **before** joining on **adjacent Motif** and slip st in ch-sp of next Picot (second Picot **before** joining), [ch 1, slip st in next ch on **new Motif** to form Picot, dc in ring, ch 3, slip st in third ch from hook (**Picot made**), dc in ring, ch 1, skip joining and next Picot on **adjacent Motif** and slip st in ch-sp of next Picot (second Picot **after** joining)] twice, pull yarn tail to close, ch 1, slip st in next ch on **new Motif** to form last Picot; join with slip st to third ch of beginning ch-6, finish off: 12 Picots.

Fig. 18a

Fig. 18b

Posies
Cowl

While making this cowl, you will learn how to:

- Begin your motif with a chain ring

- Join to the first stitch when working in rounds

- Join a new color of yarn

- Work a no-sew joining to connect your motifs together as you crochet the last round

- Follow a diagram for motif placement

EASY +

Finished Size:

Approximately 12" high x 32" circumference

(30.5 cm x 81.5 cm)

──── SHOPPING LIST ────

Yarn (Medium Weight) 🧶 **4** MEDIUM

[3.5 ounces, 170 yards

(100 grams, 156 meters) per skein**]**:

☐ Color A (Pink) - 1 skein

☐ Color B (Dk Pink) - 1 skein

Crochet Hook

☐ Size I (5.5 mm) **or** size needed for gauge

GAUGE INFORMATION

Gauge Swatch: 4" (10 cm) diameter

Work same as First Motif: 6 Petals.

──── STITCH GUIDE ────

🎥 **TREBLE CROCHET** *(abbreviated tr)*

YO twice, insert hook in st indicated, YO

and pull up a loop (4 loops on hook), (YO

and draw through 2 loops on hook) 3 times.

INSTRUCTIONS
First Motif

With Color A, ch 4; 📹 join with slip st to first ch made to form a ring *(Fig. 19)*.

Fig. 19

Rnd 1 (Right side)**:** Ch 3 **(counts as first dc),** 📹 11 dc in ring *(Fig. 20a)*; 📹 join with slip st to first dc *(Fig. 20b)*, finish off: 12 dc.

Fig. 20a

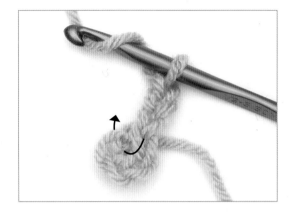

Fig. 20b

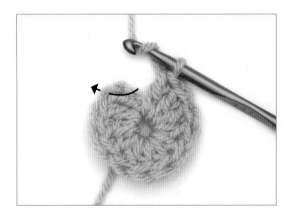

Note: Loop a short piece of yarn around any stitch to mark Rnd 1 as **right** side.

Let nature be your guide in planning the colors of your flower centers and petals.

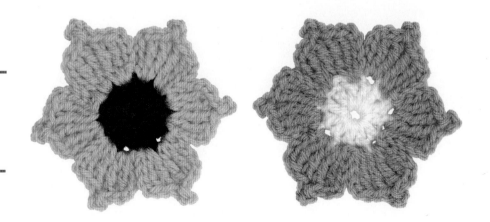

Rnd 2: With **right** side facing, 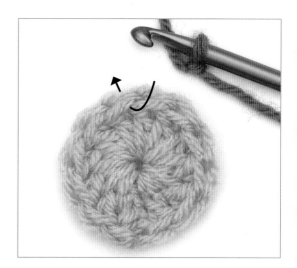 join Color B with slip st in any dc *(Fig. 21a & b)*; ch 4, 2 tr in same st as joining, ch 3, slip st in third ch from hook (**Picot made**), (2 tr, ch 4, slip st) in next dc, ★ (slip st, ch 4, 2 tr) in next dc, ch 3, slip st in third ch from hook (**Picot made**), (2 tr, ch 4, slip st) in next dc; repeat from ★ around; finish off: 6 Petals.

Fig. 21a

Fig. 21b

SECOND MOTIF

With Color A, ch 4; join with slip st to form a ring.

Rnd 1 (Right side)**:** Ch 3 (**counts as first dc**), 11 dc in ring; join with slip st to first dc, finish off: 12 dc.

Note: Mark Rnd 1 as **right** side.

🎥 The method used to connect the Motifs is a no-sew joining known as "join-as-you-go."

Insert your hook from the **back** to the **front** through the ch-sp of any Picot on the **adjacent Motif**, keeping the working yarn at the **back** of your hook.

Rnd 2 (Joining rnd)**:** With **right** side facing, join Color B with slip st in any dc; ch 4, 2 tr in same st as joining, ★ ch 3, slip st in third ch from hook (**Picot made**), (2 tr, ch 4, slip st) in next dc, (slip st, ch 4, 2 tr) in next dc; repeat from ★ 4 times **more**, ch 1; holding Motifs with **right** side facing, slip st in ch-sp of any Picot on **First Motif** *(Fig. 22a)*, ch 1, slip st in next ch on **Second Motif** to form last Picot *(Fig. 22b)*, (2 tr, ch 4, slip st) in last dc; join with slip st to joining slip st, finish off: 6 Petals.

Fig. 22a

Fig. 22b

Motifs 3 thru 18

With Color A, ch 4; join with slip st to form a ring.

Rnd 1 (Right side)**:** Ch 3 (**counts as first dc**), 11 dc in ring; join with slip st to first dc, finish off: 12 dc.

Note: Mark Rnd 1 as **right** side.

Refer to Diagram for Motif Placement and order. Continue inserting your hook from the **back** to the **front** through the ch-sp of Picot indicated on the **adjacent Motif**, keeping the working yarn at the **back** of your hook.

Rnd 2 (Joining rnd)**:** With **right** side facing, join Color B with slip st in any dc; ch 4, 2 tr in same st as joining, ★ ch 3, slip st in third ch from hook (**Picot made**), (2 tr, ch 4, slip st) in next dc, (slip st, ch 4, 2 tr) in next dc; repeat from ★ 3 times **more**, † ch 1; holding Motifs with **right** side facing, slip st in ch-sp of Picot on **adjacent Motif**, ch 1, slip st in next ch on **new Motif** to form Picot, (2 tr, ch 4, slip st) in next dc †, (slip st, ch 4, 2 tr) in next dc, repeat from † to † once; join with slip st to joining slip st, finish off: 6 Petals.

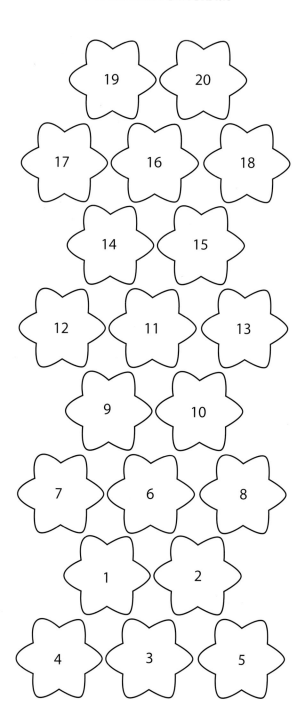

Motif 19

With Color A, ch 4; join with slip st to form a ring.

Rnd 1 (Right side)**:** Ch 3 (**counts as first dc**), 11 dc in ring; join with slip st to first dc, finish off: 12 dc.

Note: Mark Rnd 1 as **right** side.

This Motif is joined to the adjacent Motifs in the following order: Motif 17, Motif 16, Motif 3, Motif 4.

Rnd 2 (Joining rnd)**:** With **right** side facing, join Color B with slip st in any dc; ch 4, 2 tr in same st as joining, ch 3, slip st in third ch from hook (**Picot made**), (2 tr, ch 4, slip st) in next dc, † (slip st, ch 4, 2 tr) in next dc, ch 1; holding Motifs with **right** side facing, slip st in ch-sp of Picot on **adjacent Motif**, ch 1, slip st in next ch on **new Motif** to form Picot, (2 tr, ch 4, slip st) in next dc †; repeat from † to † once **more**, (slip st, ch 4, 2 tr) in next dc, ch 3, slip st in third ch from hook (**Picot made**), (2 tr, ch 4, slip st) in next dc, repeat from † to † twice; join with slip st to joining slip st, finish off: 6 Petals.

Motif 20

With Color A, ch 4; join with slip st to form a ring.

Rnd 1 (Right side)**:** Ch 3 (**counts as first dc**), 11 dc in ring; join with slip st to first dc, finish off: 12 dc.

Note: Mark Rnd 1 as **right** side.

This Motif is joined to the adjacent Motifs in the following order: Motif 5, Motif 3, Motif 19, Motif 16, Motif 18.

Rnd 2 (Joining rnd)**:** With **right** side facing, join Color B with slip st in any dc; ch 4, 2 tr in same st as joining, ch 3, slip st in third ch from hook (**Picot made**), (2 tr, ch 4, slip st) in next dc, ★ (slip st, ch 4, 2 tr) in next dc, ch 1; holding Motifs with **right** side facing, slip st in ch-sp of Picot on **adjacent Motif**, ch 1, slip st in next ch on **new Motif** to form Picot, (2 tr, ch 4, slip st) in next dc; repeat from ★ 4 times **more**; join with slip st to joining slip st, finish off: 6 Petals.

The airy joining pattern of these motifs helps to highlight the shapes of the individual flowers.

General
Instructions

ABBREVIATIONS

ch(s)	chain(s)
cm	centimeters
dc	double crochet(s)
hdc	half double crochet(s)
mm	millimeters
Rnd(s)	Round(s)
sc	single crochet(s)
sp(s)	space(s)
st(s)	stitch(es)
tr	treble crochet(s)
YO	yarn over

SYMBOLS & TERMS

★ — work instructions following ★ as many **more** times as indicated in addition to the first time.

† to † — work all instructions from first † to second † **as many** times as specified.

( ) or [ ] — work enclosed instructions **as many** times as specified by the number immediately following **or** work all enclosed instructions in the stitch or space indicated **or** contains explanatory remarks.

colon (:) — the number(s) given after a colon at the end of a round denote(s) the number of stitches or spaces you should have on that round.

▰▱▱▱ **BEGINNER**	Projects for first-time crocheters using basic stitches. Minimal shaping.
▰▰▱▱ **EASY**	Projects using yarn with basic stitches, repetitive stitch patterns, simple color changes, and simple shaping and finishing.
▰▰▰▱ **INTERMEDIATE**	Projects using a variety of techniques, such as basic lace patterns or color patterns, mid-level shaping and finishing.
▰▰▰▰ **EXPERIENCED**	Projects with intricate stitch patterns, techniques and dimension, such as non-repeating patterns, multi-color techniques, fine threads, small hooks, detailed shaping and refined finishing.

CROCHET TERMINOLOGY		
UNITED STATES		INTERNATIONAL
slip stitch (slip st)	=	single crochet (sc)
single crochet (sc)	=	double crochet (dc)
half double crochet (hdc)	=	half treble crochet (htr)
double crochet (dc)	=	treble crochet(tr)
treble crochet (tr)	=	double treble crochet (dtr)
double treble crochet (dtr)	=	triple treble crochet (ttr)
triple treble crochet (tr tr)	=	quadruple treble crochet (qtr)
skip	=	miss

GAUGE

Exact gauge is essential for proper size. Before beginning your project, make the sample swatch given in the individual instructions in the yarn and hook specified. After completing the swatch, measure it, counting your stitches and rounds carefully. If your swatch is larger or smaller than specified, **make another, changing hook size to get the correct gauge.** Keep trying until you find the size hook that will give you the specified gauge.

Yarn Weight Symbol & Names	LACE (0)	SUPER FINE (1)	FINE (2)	LIGHT (3)	MEDIUM (4)	BULKY (5)	SUPER BULKY (6)
Type of Yarns in Category	Fingering, 10-count crochet thread	Sock, Fingering Baby	Sport, Baby	DK, Light Worsted	Worsted, Afghan, Aran	Chunky, Craft, Rug	Bulky, Roving
Crochet Gauge* Ranges in Single Crochet to 4" (10 cm)	32-42 double crochets**	21-32 sts	16-20 sts	12-17 sts	11-14 sts	8-11 sts	5-9 sts
Advised Hook Size Range	Steel*** 6,7,8 Regular hook B-1	B-1 to E-4	E-4 to 7	7 to I-9	I-9 to K-10.5	K-10.5 to M-13	M-13 and larger

*GUIDELINES ONLY: The chart above reflects the most commonly used gauges and hook sizes for specific yarn categories.

** Lace weight yarns are usually crocheted on larger-size hooks to create lacy openwork patterns. Accordingly, a gauge range is difficult to determine. Always follow the gauge stated in your pattern.

*** Steel crochet hooks are sized differently from regular hooks–the higher the number the smaller the hook, which is the reverse of regular hook sizing.

CROCHET HOOKS																
U.S.	B-1	C-2	D-3	E-4	F-5	G-6	7	H-8	I-9	J-10	K-10½	L-11	M/N-13	N/P-15	P/Q	Q	S
Metric - mm	2.25	2.75	3.25	3.5	3.75	4	4.5	5	5.5	6	6.5	8	9	10	15	16	19

Yarn
Information

The projects in this book were made using Medium Weight Yarn. Any brand of Medium Weight Yarn may be used. It is best to refer to the yardage/meters when determining how many balls or skeins to purchase. Remember, to arrive at the finished size, it is the GAUGE/TENSION that is important, not the brand of yarn. For your convenience, listed below are the specific yarns used to create our photography models.

TRADITIONAL GRANNY AFGHAN
Lion Brand® Vanna's Choice®
White - #100 White
Red - #113 Scarlet
Blue - #109 Colonial Blue

AMISH HEXAGON AFGHAN
Lion Brand® Vanna's Choice®
Dusty Purple - #146 Dusty Purple
Magenta - #144 Magenta
Dusty Rose - #140 Dusty Rose

BLOOMING SQUARES BABY AFGHAN
Lion Brand® Vanna's Choice® Baby
Melon - #132 Goldfish
Lt Green - #168 Mint
Yellow - #157 Duckie

AUTUMN MUMS SHAWL
Lion Brand® Vanna's Choice®
Brown - #126 Chocolate
Lt Blue - #105 Silver Blue
Navy - #110 Navy
Lt Tan - #099 Linen

FRILLY CIRCLES SCARF
Lion Brand® Vanna's Choice®
Bright Purple - #145 Eggplant
Blue - #109 Colonial Blue
Lt Blue - #105 Silver Blue
Purple - #147 Purple

POSIES COWL
Lion Brand® Vanna's Choice®
Pink - #101 Pink
Dk Pink - #112 Raspberry